Purple Snowflakes and Titty Wanks

Written and performed by Sarah Hanly

CAST

Saoirse **Sarah Hanly**

Director **Alice Fitzgerald**
Designer **Jacob Lucy**
Lighting Designer **Elliot Griggs**
Sound Designer **Alexandra Faye Braithwaite**
Associate Designer **Anna Kelsey**
Movement Director **Rachael Nanyonjo**
Drama Therapist **Nikki Disney**
Intimacy Director **Yarit Dor**
Stage Managers **Sophia Dalton, Bronagh Doherty**
Set Construction **Quiver**
Propmaking **Dylan Farrell**

For the Royal Court:

Company Manager **Joni Carter**
Stage Supervisor **TJ Chappell-Meade**
Production Manager **Marius Rønning**
Lead Producer **Catherine Thornborrow**
Costume Supervisor **Katie Price**
Lighting Supervisor **Johnny Wilson**

For the Abbey Theatre:

Producer **Craig Flaherty**
Production Manager **Andy Keogh**
Head of Lighting **Kevin McFadden**
Head of Sound **Morgan Dunne**
Producing Assistant **Clara Purcell**

The Royal Court Theatre, Abbey Theatre and Stage Management wish to thank the following
for their help with this production: Damian Gildea
and would also like to thank Dóchas Pictures for its support and charitable outreach.

Purple Snowflakes and Titty Wanks
Written and performed by Sarah Hanly

Sarah Hanly (Writer/Performer)

As writer/performer, theatre includes: **Purple Snowflakes and Titty Wanks (Abbey, Dublin/ Leicester Square/Southwark/Above the Arts/ Theatre N16).**

As writer, theatre includes: **SHOWER [part of Dear Ireland programme] (Abbey, Dublin).**

As performer, theatre includes: **One Minute (Barn, Cirencester); The Penelopiad (Jacksons Lane); London Irish Showcase (Abbey, Dublin/Tristan Bates); Moscow State Circus (Bord Gáis Energy); McDonald's 40th Anniversary (Excel London).**

Film includes: **The Hole in the Ground, Rebirth (short), There They're Their (short), Dogs of War (Shakespeare Shorts).**

Sarah was the 2019 recipient of the Pinter Commission for her new play set in Ireland during the War of Independence.

Alexandra Faye Braithwaite
(Sound Designer)

Theatre includes: **Purple Snowflakes and Titty Wanks (Abbey, Dublin); Groan Ups (West End/ UK Tour); Bloody Elle, Wuthering Heights, Light Falls (Royal Exchange, Manchester); Home I'm Darling (Stephen Joseph/Octagon, Bolton/ Theatre By The Lake); Neville's Island (Queen's, Hornchurch); The Audience, Juicy & Delicious (Nuffield, Southampton); Toast (The Other Palace/Lowry/Traverse); Hamlet, Talking Heads, Rudolph (Leeds Playhouse); Things of Dry Hours (Young Vic); Cougar, Dealing With Clair, The Rolling Stone (Orange Tree); A Christmas Carol (Theatr Clwyd); Romeo & Juliet (China Plate); Acceptance (Hampstead); Chicken Soup (Crucible, Sheffield); Dublin Carol (Sherman, Cardiff); Kanye the First (HighTide Festival); Room (& Theatre Royal, Stratford East), The Remains of Maisie Duggan (Abbey, Dublin); If I Was Queen (Almeida); The Tempest (Royal & Derngate, Northampton); Diary of a Madman (Gate/Traverse); Simon Slack (Soho); Happy To Help (Park); The Future (Yard); My Beautiful Black Dog (Southbank Centre); Hamlet is Dead, No Gravity (Arcola); Remote (Theatre Royal, Plymouth); Lonely Soldiers (Arts); Grumpy Old Women III (UK tour).**

Nikki Disney (Drama Therapist)

Nikki is a state registered Drama psychotherapist, Clinical Supervisor (MA. HCPC, Badth), theatre director and yoga teacher who has worked with vulnerable groups and individuals using art for over 16 years. She has implemented and delivered Safeguarding and wellbeing procedures within arts organisations, lead on access and wellbeing for The Party Somewhere Else festival and trained artists on boundaries, trauma informed approaches and wellbeing with organisations such as Derby theatre and JMK. She has implemented tool kits for wellbeing in the rehearsal room and advised on implementing wellbeing strategies throughout institutions.

Nikki is the founder of Stage Weight Wellbeing, which focus on consultation around artist wellbeing during the rehearsal process specialising in themes of trauma, mental health and autobiographical material. Recent ACE funded R&D projects include Aunting, Bonfires, Princess Charming, Inside Voice, Bonkers, Fandom, Summer Camp for Broken People, Enter with Boldness and Widows. She has offered 1:1 therapeutic support on projects with Regent's Park Theatre, Nottingham Playhouse and CBBC.

Alice Fitzgerald (Director)

Theatre includes: **Purple Snowflakes and Titty Wanks (Abbey, Dublin/Leicester Square/ Southwark/Above the Arts/Theatre N16); Sharp [audio play] (Bitter Pill); Bonfire [R&D] (Déda); In Vitro Veritas (Karamel Club); [scenes from] The Kitchen Sink (Edinburgh Fringe Festival).**

As assistant director, theatre includes: **Brixton Rock (The Big House); Clybourne Park (Karamel Club); Merit (Finborough).**

Dramaturgy includes: **Maiden Speech Festival (Tristan Bates).**

Elliot Griggs (Lighting Designer)

For the Royal Court: **Living Newspaper, On Bear Ridge (& National Theatre Wales), Yen (& Royal Exchange, Manchester).**

Other theatre includes: **Purple Snowflakes and Titty Wanks (Abbey, Dublin); Amélie the Musical (The Other Palace/Watermill/ West End/UK Tour); Fleabag (Soho/ Edinburgh Festival Fringe/ West End/SoHo Playhouse, NYC/Tour); The Wild Duck (Almeida); The Lover/The Collection (West End); An Octoroon (& National), The Sugar Syndrome, Low Level Panic, Sheppey, buckets (Orange Tree); Missing Julie (Theatr Clwyd); Ivan & the Dogs (Young Vic); Richard III (Headlong); Disco Pigs (West End/Irish Rep, NYC); Acceptance, Dry Powder, Diminished (Hampstead); Pomona (& Orange Tree/ National), Queens of the Coal Age, The Night Watch (Royal Exchange, Manchester); Missing People (Leeds Playhouse/Kani Public Arts, Japan); Psychodrama (Never For Ever); Blue Door (Ustinov Studio); Loot (Park/Watermill); Somnium (Sadlers Wells); Hir (Bush); Fool For Love (Found111); Lampedusa (HighTide); The Oracles (Punchdrunk); Martha, Josie & the Chinese Elvis, Educating Rita (Hull Truck); Shift, Bromance (Barely Methodical Troupe).**

Live events include: **Lost Lagoon, Height of Winter, The Single-Opticon, Alcoholic Architecture (Bompas & Parr).**

Awards include: **Off West End Award for Best Lighting Designer (Pomona).**

Anna Kelsey (Associate Designer)

As designer, theatre includes: **The Wicker Husband, Under Milk Wood, Our Town (Watermill); Microwave (Run Amok); The Sorcerers Apprentice (Southwark Playhouse); The Man Who Wanted to be a Penguin (Stuff & Nonsense); Charmane (Raised Eyebrows); Exodus (Motherlode); Guesthouse (Eastern Angles); Moby Dick the Musical (Union); Shirley Valentine (Lighthouse); The Great American Trailer Park Musical (Waterloo East); 1001 Nights (Queens, Hornchurch).**

As associate designer, theatre includes: **Purple Snowflakes and Titty Wanks (Abbey, Dublin).**

As assistant designer, theatre includes: **The Boy in the Dress, Measure for Measure, Venice Preserved, Kunene & the King (RSC).**

Anna was Resident Assistant Designer with the Royal Shakespeare Company 2018–2019 and is a Creative Associate for the Watermill Theatre.

Jacob Lucy (Designer)

As designer, theatre includes: **Purple Snowflakes and Titty Wanks (Abbey, Dublin); The End Of History (High Hearted, St Giles-In-The- Fields); The Enchanted (Bunker); Brixton Rock (Big House).**

As co-scenographer, theatre includes: **Neverland (Parco Corsini, Italy).**

Rachael Nanyonjo
(Movement Director)

As choreographer/movement director, theatre includes: **Purple Snowflakes and Titty Wanks (Abbey, Dublin); Changing Destiny, In a Word, American Dream (Young Vic); The Death of a Black Man, Either (Hampstead); Pigeon English (Bristol School of Acting); Cinderella (Nottingham Playhouse); Spine (UK Tour); Great Expectations (& Southwark Playhouse), After It Rains (NYT); Two Trains Running (ETT/Royal & Derngate, Northampton); Does My Bomb Look Big In This (Soho/Tara Arts); Babylon Beyond Borders (Bush); Macbeth (Orange Tree); The Jumper Factory (Young Vic/Bristol Old Vic); Misty (West End); Shebeen (& Nottingham Playhouse), Sleeping Beauty (Theatre Royal, Stratford East); Bernstein's Mass (Southbank Centre); Twilight (Gate); The Divide, Cover My Tracks (Old Vic).**

As director, theatre includes: **Recognition [audio play] (45North/Ellie Keel Productions); Bobsleigh [Old Vic Monologues] (Old Vic); An Alternative Musical [NT Learning – codirector] (National); Assata – She Who Struggles [Young Vic fresh direction] (Young Vic); 2:1 (Kanzaze Dance).**

As associate director, theatre includes: **Moonlight/ Night School (West End); Pericles [Public Acts First Stage] (National).**

As assistant director, theatre includes: **The Step Mother, Caroline Or Change (Chichester Festival); Underwater Love (Arcola/Clapham Omnibus); Kayla (Young Vic).**

As choreographer, television includes: **The Statistical Probability Of Love At First Sight, Cbeebies, Cbeebies: Christmas In Storyland, Pirates. As director, film includes: Amazina.**

THE ROYAL COURT THEATRE

The Royal Court Theatre is the writers' theatre. It is a leading force in world theatre for cultivating and supporting writers – undiscovered, emerging and established.

Through the writers, the Royal Court is at the forefront of creating restless, alert, provocative theatre about now. We open our doors to the unheard voices and free thinkers that, through their writing, change our way of seeing.

Over 120,000 people visit the Royal Court in Sloane Square, London, each year and many thousands more see our work elsewhere through transfers to the West End and New York, UK and international tours, digital platforms, our residencies across London, and our site-specific work. Through all our work we strive to inspire audiences and influence future writers with radical thinking and provocative discussion.

The Royal Court's extensive development activity encompasses a diverse range of writers and artists and includes an ongoing programme of writers' attachments, readings, workshops and playwriting groups. Twenty years of the International Department's pioneering work around the world means the Royal Court has relationships with writers on every continent.

Since 1956 we have commissioned and produced hundreds of writers, from John Osborne to Jasmine Lee-Jones. Royal Court plays from every decade are now performed on stage and taught in classrooms and universities across the globe.

We're now working to the future and are committed to becoming carbon net zero and ensuring we are a just, equitable, transparent and ethical cultural space - from our anti-oppression work, to our relationship with freelancers, to credible climate pledges.

It is because of this commitment to the writer and our future that we believe there is no more important theatre in the world than the Royal Court.

Find out more at royalcourttheatre.com

 royalcourt royalcourttheatre

Supported using public funding by
ARTS COUNCIL ENGLAND

ROYAL COURT SUPPORTERS

The Royal Court relies on its supporters in addition to our core grant from Arts Council England and our ticket sales. We are particularly grateful to the individuals, trusts and companies who stood by us and continued to support our work during these recent difficult times. It is with this vital support that the Royal Court remains the writers' theatre and that we can continue to seek out, develop and nurture new voices, both on and off our stages.

Thank you to all who support the Royal Court in this way. We really can't do it without you.

PUBLIC FUNDING

CHARITABLE PARTNERS

BackstageTrust

JERWOOD ARTS

ORANGE TREE TRUST

CORPORATE SPONSORS

Aqua Financial Ltd
Cadogan
Colbert
Edwardian Hotels, London
SISTER

CORPORATE MEMBERS

Platinum
Auriens
Bloomberg Philanthropies

Silver
Left Bank Pictures
Patrizia
Sloane Stanley

TRUSTS & FOUNDATIONS

The Derrill Allatt Foundation
The Backstage Trust
Martin Bowley Charitable Trust
The City Bridge Trust
The Cleopatra Trust
Cockayne – Grants for the Arts
The Noël Coward Foundation
Cowley Charitable Foundation
The D'Oyly Carte Charitable Trust
Edgerton Foundation
Garrick Charitable Trust
The Golden Bottle Trust
Jerwood Arts
Kirsh Foundation
The London Community Foundation
Claire McIntyre's Bursary
Lady Antonia Fraser for the Pinter Commission
Richard Radcliffe Charitable Trust
Rose Foundation
Royal Victoria Hall Foundation
The Charles Skey Charitable Trust
John Thaw Foundation
The Thistle Trust
The Victoria Wood Foundation

To find out more about supporting the Royal Court please get in touch with the Development Team at support@royalcourttheatre.com, call 020 7565 5030 or visit royalcourttheatre.com/support-us

Abbey Theatre | Amharclann na Mainistreach

Located right in the heart of Dublin, the Abbey Theatre is Ireland's National Theatre. It was founded by W. B. Yeats and Lady Augusta Gregory. Since it first opened its doors in 1904 the theatre has played a vital role in the artistic, social and cultural life of Ireland.

It may be steeped in history but its year-round programme is a great mix of modern and classic plays from both Irish and international artists. There is also a wide variety of art forms, and on a given night you might also find dance, opera, music and literary performances on either of its two stages.

Inspired by the revolutionary ideals of its founders and its rich canon of Irish dramatic writing, the Abbey Theatre's mission is to imaginatively engage with all Irish society through the production of ambitious, courageous and new theatre in all its forms. The Abbey Theatre commits to lead in the telling of the whole Irish story, in English and in Irish, and affirms that it is a theatre for the entire island of Ireland and for all its people. In every endeavour, the Abbey Theatre promotes inclusiveness, diversity and equality.

The Abbey Theatre gratefully acknowledges the support of the Arts Council.

ABBEY THEATRE SUPPORTERS

PRINCIPAL PARTNER

PROGRAMME PARTNERS

CORPORATE GUARDIANS

GOLD AMBASSADORS
Behaviour and Attitudes

SILVER AMBASSADORS
Trocadero

DIRECTORS' CIRCLE
Tony Ahearne
Richard and Sherril Burrows
Pat Butler
The Cielinski Family
Deirdre Finan
Donal Moore
Sheelagh O'Neill
Dr. Frances Ruane
Susan and Denis Tinsley
Lloyd Weinreb

SILVER PATRONS
Frances Britton
Tommy Gibbons
Dr. John Keane
Andrew Mackey
Eugenie Mackey
Eugene Magee
Gerard and Liv McNaughton
The Kathleen Murphy Foundation

ABBEY THEATRE STAFF

Andrea Ainsworth
Donal Ayton
Cliff Barragry
Johanna Bear
Roxzan Bowes
Maeubh Brennan
Susan Bryan
Nicola Burke
Orla Burke
Simon Burke
Eoin Byrne
Maura Campbell
David Carpenter
Daire Cavanagh
Owen Vincent
Clarke
Conall Coleman
Derek Conaghy
Lilly Conlon
Evan Connolly
Jeff Conway
Jen Coppinger
Karl Corr
Fiona Cradock
Kate Crook
Richard Curwood
Sophia Dalton
Deirdre Daly
Mairéad Delaney
Clarissa Delap
Karima Dillon
Pat Dillon
Debbie Doak
Bronagh Doherty
Colin Doran
Con Doyle
Laura Doyle
Ken Dunne
Morgan Dunne
Danny Erskine
Breege Fahy
Dylan Farrell
Eimear Farrell
Lisa Farrelly
Kate Finn
John Finnegan
Craig Flaherty

Neasa Flannery
Ellen Fleming
Robert Flynn
Veronica Foo
Tara Furlong
Sophie Furlong
Tighe
Derek Garland
Brendan Galvin
Donna Geraghty
Catherine Griffin
John Gunning
Fergus Hannigan
Grace Healy
Brenda Herbert
Daniel Hickey
William Hickey
Dermot Hicks
James Hickson
Dara Hogan
Laura Honan
Philip Hughes
Narges Jahani
Vlatka Jeh
Larry Jones
Izzy Jones-McAuley
Sarah Jones
Muireann Kane
Maeve Keane
Conor Kelly
Fergus Kelly
Yvonne Kelly
Ailbhe Kelly-Miller
Tom Kennedy
Shane Kenny
Andy Keogh
Phil Kingston
Michael Kyle
Luke Lamont
Marie Lawlor
Tim Leech–Cleary
Adrian Leake
Patrick Lehane
Ciara Lynch
Bridget Lynskey
Faust
Julia MacConville

Darren Magnier
Scott Maguire
Stephen Maguire
Claire Maher
Heather Maher
Elaine Mannion
Éadaoin McCarrick
Davy McChrystal
Aoife McCollum
Dan McDermott
Kevin McFadden
Róisín McGann
Aidan McGillan
Ciaran McGlynn
Terence McGoff
Grace McKiernan
Caitríona McLaughlin
Gus McNamara
Victoria Miller
Christine Monk
Nadine-Mary Moore
Adrian Moylan
Conor Mullan
Tara Mulvihill
Aoife Murphy
Donna Murphy
Eimer Murphy
Kathyann Murphy
Orlagh Murphy
Agnieszka Myszka
Marykerin Naughton
Emily Ní Bhroin
Síofra Ní Chiardha
Pawel Nieworaj
Mark O'Brien
Adam O'Connell
Esther O'Connor
Colin O'Connor
Jack O'Dea
Tara O'Reilly
Emma-Kate O'Reilly
Selina O'Reilly
Simon O'Reilly
Valentina Quiroga
Laura Rainsford
Martin Reid
Dean Reidy

Fiona Reynolds
Zoë Reynolds
Seán Roper Nolan
Audrey Rooney
Josh Roxby
Pat Russell
Barbara Ryan
Aidah Sama
Joe Sanders
Andrew Smith
Rían Smith
Sarah Smith
Sharon Sorohan
Fergal Styles
Seán Treacy
Leanne Vaughey
Sean Walsh
Jesse Weaver
Sarah-Jane Williams
Sally Withnell
Monika Wlodarczyk
Bill Woodland
Damien Woods
Diarmuid Woods

BOARD

Noelle Brown
Mairéad Delaney
Múirne Laffan
Máire O'Higgins
Michael Owens
Dr. Frances Ruane
(Chair)
Owen Travers
Michael Wall
Michael West

ROYAL

BAR & KITCHEN

The Royal Court's Bar & Kitchen aims to create a welcoming and inspiring environment with a style and ethos that reflects the work we put on stage.

Offering expertly crafted cocktails alongside an extensive selection of craft gins and beers, wine and soft drinks, our vibrant basement bar provides a sanctuary in the middle of Sloane Square. By day a perfect spot for meetings or quiet reflection and by night atmospheric meeting spaces for cast, crew, audiences and the general public.

All profits go directly to supporting the work of the Royal Court theatre, cultivating and supporting writers – undiscovered, emerging and established.

For more information, visit
royalcourttheatre.com/bar

HIRES & EVENTS

The Royal Court is available to hire for celebrations, rehearsals, meetings, filming, ceremonies and much more. Our two theatre spaces can be hired for conferences and showcases, and the building is a unique venue for bespoke events and receptions.

For more information, visit
royalcourttheatre.com/events

Sloane Square London, SW1W 8AS ⊖ Sloane Square ⇌ Victoria Station
🐦 royalcourt 👍 theroyalcourttheatre 📷 royalcourttheatre

COURT

SUPPORT THE COURT AND BE A PART OF OUR FUTURE.

Every penny raised goes directly towards producing bold new writing for our stages, cultivating and supporting writers in the UK and around the world, and inspiring the next generation of theatre-makers.

You can make a one-off donation by text:

Text **Support 5** to 70560 to donate £5

Text **Support 10** to 70560 to donate £10

Text **Support 20** to 70560 to donate £20

Texts cost the donation amount plus one standard message. UK networks only.

To find out more about the different ways in which you can get involved, visit our website: royalcourttheatre.com/support-us

The English Stage Company at the Royal Court Theatre is a registered charity (No. 231242)

Purple Snowflakes and Titty Wanks

Sarah Hanly is a writer, actress and owner of the production company Dóchas Pictures. As writer, theatre includes: *Shower* (as part of *Dear Ireland*, Abbey Theatre, Dublin). As performer, theatre includes: *One Minute* (Barn, Cirencester); *The Penelopiad* (Jacksons Lane); London Irish Showcase (Abbey, Dublin/Tristan Bates); Moscow State Circus (Bord Gáis Energy); McDonald's 40th Anniversary (Excel London). Film includes: *The Hole in the Ground*, *Rebirth* (short), *There They're Their* (short) and *Dogs of War* (Shakespeare Shorts). Sarah was the 2019 recipient of the Pinter Commission for her new play set in Ireland during the War of Independence. Sarah is currently working on commissions for theatre and television. Dóchas Pictures will produce television, film and theatre projects.

SARAH HANLY

Purple Snowflakes
and Titty Wanks

and

Shower

faber

First published in 2021
by Faber and Faber Limited
74–77 Great Russell Street
London WC1B 3DA

This edition, with revisions, was first published in 2022

Typeset by Brighton Gray
Printed and bound in the UK by CPI Group (Ltd), Croydon CR0 4YY

A CIP record for this book
is available from the British Library

978-0-571-37754-1

2 4 6 8 10 9 7 5 3 1

Contents

Acknowledgements

Many thanks to:

Vicky Featherstone
Jane Fallowfield
Mel Kenyon
Alice Fitzgerald
Lucy Davies
Catherine Thornborrow
Everyone at the Royal Court Theatre
Caitríona McLaughlin
Mark O'Brien
Jen Coppinger
Craig Flaherty
Neil Murray
All the team at the Abbey Theatre
Dinah Wood and Jodi Gray at Faber & Faber for their
patience and understanding
Nick de Somogyi
Leo Butler and the Royal Court writers' group
Imogen Sarre, Casarotto Ramsay & Associates
The Old Diorama Arts Centre, Peter James CBE
The Eating Disorder Charity, Beat
Lexi Clare, Emma Hall and John Brant
Nikki Disney
Damian Gildea
Bronagh Doherty & Sophia Dalton
Elliot Griggs, Jacob Lucy, Alexandra Faye Braithwaite, Rachael
Nanyonjo, Yarit Dor, Joni Carter and all the team
Jacqui Somerville, Sherrill Gow, Kristina Kapadocha and all at
Mountview Academy of Theatre Arts
Maddie Rice, Jasmine Lee-Jones and Debris Stevenson
Peter, Catherine, Elizabeth, Dermot, Luc and all at home in
London and Éire too.

PURPLE SNOWFLAKES AND TITTY WANKS

For women gone before, coming behind, and those here by my side, for my sisters, everywhere.

To Vicky, Mel and Dinah.

Purple Snowflakes and Titty Wanks was first performed in a co-production at the Abbey Theatre, Dublin, on 30 September 2021, and at the Royal Court Jerwood Theatre Upstairs, London, on 1 February 2022. The cast and creative team was as follows.

Saoirse Sarah Hanly

Director Alice Fitzgerald
Designer Jacob Lucy
Lighting Designer Elliot Griggs
Sound Designer Alexandra Faye Braithwaite
Associate Designer Anna Kelsey
Movement Director Rachael Nanyonjo
Drama Therapist Nikki Disney
Intimacy Director Yarit Dor
Stage Managers Sophia Dalton, Bronagh Doherty
Set Construction Quiver
Propmaking Dylan Farrell

For the Abbey Theatre:
Producer Craig Flaherty
Production Manager Andy Keogh
Head of Lighting Kevin McFadden
Head of Sound Morgan Dunne
Producing Assistant Clara Purcell

For the Royal Court:
Company Manager Joni Carter
Stage Supervisor TJ Chappell-Meade
Production Manager Marius Rønning
Lead Producer Catherine Thornborrow
Costume Supervisor Katie Price
Lighting Supervisor Johnny Wilson

Characters

Saoirse

plays herself and the other characters, too:
Ashling
Séamus
Father Mick
Daisy
Sister Patricia
Mrs O'Heffer
Jack O'Quiffe
Mr Glynn
Aoife Kelly
Mrs Toad
Orla
Beth
Anna
Maria
Glitzy Principal
Reverend Mother
Jacinta
Brenda
Otillie
Child
Child's Mummy
Police Officer
Nurse
Hospital Chaplain
Brendan
Pope Joan
Gabriella

A note on the text

For the purpose of solo performance, text in square brackets [ ] may be used to indicate who is speaking in the scene. Text in quotation marks ('') implies a character's speech, directed to another. Text without quotation marks may refer to Saoirse's interaction with the audience and her private dialogue with Ashling too. A forward slash (/) implies where the line is interrupted. A dash (–) indicates a beat.

Acknowledging the male hierarchy and psychological implications in the world of the play means it is important to understand how Saoirse may transcend through time and space to unveil the fog of her human existence. Beginning from presence, and ending in presence, she is at all times a living breathing human being.

The play is set in three acts and it should run all the way through.

Act One

St Maria's Enniskerry hums in an egged-cream fog. Lights come up on Saoirse, waiting.

Ashling (*intrigued*) Overly horny?

Saoirse [You ask.] You seem intrigued. Yes. [I says.]

Ashling In what way?

Saoirse [You says.] I don't know – I'm just very very horny, I don't know how else to put it.

Ashling Right, okay. Are you having the sex?

Saoirse God no! I've never had sex, Ashling! But while you've been out of school, I've learnt how to make my own orgasms.

Ashling What's an orgasm?

Saoirse Um, I don't really know how to describe it properly – but it's this feeling, that just shoots through your whole body like an electric current.

Ashling How in God's name do you make that happen?

Saoirse Practice, and determination! I can show you if you like? But you're not to tell anyone I do it, okay? Right, okay.

I use these.

Saoirse hands her a set of pearls. Ashling examines them.

Ashling You put these, inside you?

Saoirse No-way, I tried them up my bum once and I tell ya – it was some operation getting them out again. Orla taught me first, it happened by chance! We were giving each other tickles in the oratory. The holiest room in St Maria's Enniskerry. And it was really actually more the getting to the place, before actually, getting there. The journey to the –

'Yes Orla! I like that, oh, hello. I guess we could try it back there too.' I've never, but Orla has and she said it was like a grenade explosion. Someone needs to explain this, like verbally and maybe demonstrate with a fake bumhole. Is that okay to say? *Anal sex?* – Okay, let's call it – it's an anus. Weird name for a word, sounds like (*Pronounced like 'Shame-us'.*) Séamus.

And then Orla just tickles her pearls over the top of my vagina. And this sensation just rippled through my whole body, like a wave of fire and you're going to want to keep rubbing, at this point. *To keep the feeling going as long as you can!*

Ashling Shush Saoirse, the nuns will hear you.

Saoirse Ah, they're well used to us by now. [I says.] We're having them like three or four times a day, we're inundated asking to go to the toilet and I tell ye, they know we're not going for the shits and giggles.

She puts the pearls away.

Ashling Jeez Saoirse. Do they not *see you*?

Saoirse Gosh no – though they could probably do with having a feckin look themselves! You can borrow the pearls if you like?

–

My father left a few years ago. He just fucking vanished so we held a fake funeral for him. But the truth was, we hadn't a clue where he went. And it'd be a sin to live in a house without a *paternal law* so we tell the neighbours –

'Sudden, very sudden. Well, gradual decline and then boom, he departed.'

Séamus 'Sorry is he dead or alive?'

Saoirse [A neighbour says.] 'Yeye, I think so.'

Father Mick 'You're either one or the other, death is finite.'

Saoirse [Father Mick says.] Friend of the family, and our mum's been living with him, ever since.

Ashling Your mum lives with a priest?

Saoirse Yeye Ashling. Say nothing to no one though because it would cause holy feckin war, wouldn't it?

It fucking would.

Would it?

So me and my sister, Daisy have been holding the fort. She's been going mad because the shower was blocked again. You see our toilet in Enniskerry had a tiny little hole and I was forever blocking the loo with a shit tonne of toilet paper. I needed it to drown out the splashing sound my vomit would make. And the shower was also clogged with cornflakes, hair and pubes so I had to move onto plastic bags after that. And I meant to flush them down the loo before, Daisy /

Daisy 'Two Dunnes Stores bags, full of puke! Ugh, why the feck are these under the stairs? You'll be sorry in a minute, don't fuck with me Saoirse. What will become of your talents if you keep doing this? Don't answer the question, it's for you to think about. And secondly, tell me two life goals right now!'

Saoirse 'Eh, I want to play a real woman in the school play.' [I says.] 'And then emigrate.'

Daisy 'You are not going anywhere till you've done the leaving cert.'

Saoirse Daisy tries to talk like a *Dublin 4*, Ashling, to fit in with her posh friends and she says I talk like a *Howiye*, but the truth is neither of us belong anywhere. And she's out the back garden there, chucking the bags of puke into the flower bed.

Daisy 'It's compost!'

Saoirse [She says.]

Ashling You make yourself sick Saoirse?

Saoirse [You says.]

Ashling That's not funny.

Saoirse Ye I know. [I says.] But it numbs the pain in my head. And I like feeling empty after.

Ashling You really shouldn't do that Saoirse.

Saoirse Ye I know.

Ashling I mean it / Saoirse.

Saoirse Yeye okay Ashling, I hear you, but you should eat, something. [I says.]

–

'We made a deal here.' [He says.]

Sister Patricia 'You made a deal where?'

Saoirse [Sister Patricia says.] Yeno the sub-teacher who we bring wild stories to? I think she likes the talk, pretends she doesn't but she always sits wide-eyed and still. And we are the queen time wasters so . . .

[Dónal Flynn says.] '*We made a deal here*, Sister. *If I made you cum, you'd suck my dick*. Eh sorry Sister, whaddya call it? His willy? Penis . . . His penis Sister!'

Sister Patricia 'Oh I prefer willy it's a little less, on the tongue.'

Saoirse 'Exactly Sister now you're with me.'

Sister Patricia 'Nono I'm not going there with you! We're going back to the biology book, if you want to know about that, ask your mother.'

Saoirse 'She lives with a priest.'

Sister Patricia 'Oh, really?'

Saoirse 'Yes Sister, if you don't mind I want to tell you because I want to help you help me understand, because Dónal pushed my head down and I sucked it for a while.'

Ashling Saoirse Murphy!

Saoirse Bear with me Ashling, and she's closed her eyes.

'Are you saying a prayer for me Sister Patricia? If you're still in there Sister! I guess my question is . . . How do you pleasure a man without knowing how to?

Or if you want to? Or, how do you not prematurely climax and then lose the deal? Or just teach us to say no.'

There it is, women are conditioned to do what we're told, we are not taught how to say 'no.'

'You're really flushed sister, will I open the window? Red face. Like a big red apple.'

Yes! It's about the apple and the garden of Eden and whose sin became whose. That's what this all boils down to.

'We need to re-address the apple sinner too!'

Sister Patricia 'We do not! It was Eve's fault. She is fine as she is.'

Saoirse 'But if she is made to be a big evil whore, or a virgin, or a perfect mother and if that's *all* she can be, well then she becomes an immovable object. And I fucking move around Sister! And I need you to meet me here.'

And before I know where I am, I'm kicked out the door.

–

So I end up in front of the principal.

'I'd like the right to renegotiate my punishment.'

Mrs O'Heffer 'Ah-ah-ah-ah-ah-ah ah.'

A phone call home is made.

'Hallo there is that Mrs Murphy?

Ah, how are you Brenda?
    Listen.
    It's Máire O'Heffer here from St Maria's College
Enniskerry.
    I'm not too bad thanks Brenda –
    how are you?

Very good, now wait till I tell you. I have Saoirse here in the
office And she's actually been speaking, *sex-u-al-ly explic-it-
ly. Devil tongue!*
    Ya-ya-ya. It's nine forty-five a.m. We haven't even done
the morning Rosary yet! You know Brenda, I think there
could be some mental problems there, she's sixteen and
she's talking about cunnilingus!

No.
    It's oral sex.
    I believe. Ya-ya-ya. And we just can't handle her any
more – and she's disrupting the learning of the
    other pupils so, we're taking her out of classes and
putting her into one on her own. And a drama club, she can
exert her talents there – Okay so Brenda, we'll see you at
the school show! And how's Father Mick?

Very good, okay all the best, God bless. Bye. Bye, bye.
Byebbbbybyeebye. Bye

Brenda. Bye bbb bbbyyeebye. God bless, bye bye bye. Bye bye bye bye. Bye now. Bye bye bye bye bye. Bye bye Brenda. JESUS LOVES YOU! Bye. Bye.'

Mrs O'Heffer hangs up.

'Six weeks detention, with no trips to the toilet in any class. Or you play the King in the school play and you commit your life to the stage, the only place for your clowning. You do whatever you like with rest of your time, and then find your way into the male roles. You are too much woman for a, well *for you.*'

Saoirse 'Ugh but I wanted to be Antigone.' [I says.] 'Because she has everything taken from her. And she is like all the lead women I read about. And I want to play a real woman – and she is the realest thing I get to existing in this place . . . Can I at least be Ismene?'

Mrs O'Heffer 'Ah-ah-ah-ah-ah-Ah. Aoife Kelly is being Ismene and your sister Daisy is being Antigone. You take the King as your punishment.'

Saoirse 'Fine, I'll take the man.'

And I leave.

Brief white noise – tinnitus.

And I down my pasta in one and I head off to the loo. And I projectile the shame out of me.

The thing about pasta is it flies straight back up in one go. I avoid carbs when I'm trying to be skinny. So when I'm bingeing I have a bit of a carbohydrate party. Oh and chocolate, I fucking love chocolate. The thing about chocolate is it tastes just as good coming back up, as it does going down so I get to experience it twice. I have to be careful with cornflakes though, because if I don't let them dissolve in my tummy for long enough – they scratch my oesophagus on the way back up. I hate letting them sit there for too long though, because I'm afraid of the calories absorbing into my blood, so I put up with the pain. Well actually, I kind of like the pain. Is that weird? Oh and bread is also an awful pain in the arse to bring back up. If I don't chew it properly. It comes back up in lumps and I do be heaving over the toilet for ages. Sometimes, I just eat and spit. Chew spit chew, spit. Bread is a terrible one for creating a splash in the toilet too. If I'm not careful I get a load of sick in my eye. Fucking nightmare.

And I walk out and you're in, Ashling! You're never in. And your hair's fallen out. But your eyes are very bright.

You look well. [I says.]

Ashling Were you being sick?

Saoirse [You says.] Gosh no, I haven't done that for ages. And I eat a nibble of pasta left on the lid of my lunch box and I watch you leave for practice, I couldn't believe it, I'd never seen you in the gear before. And I watch you doing laps of the hockey pitch, your legs are covered in this downy hair, mine are too. And I spit the nibble of pasta I'd been sucking, and I slip it in my pocket, and the bodies in these uniforms, feel so restricted.

Saoirse tries to sit with it.

–

She flings her hands in the air.

(*Roaring.*) 'One More Tune! Deco's Disco!'

Music pulsates, she dances wildly.

We were like two horny devils, running from Deco's disco into the church car park night. Honest to fuck Ashling, I didn't really know what I was getting myself into.

After Jack O'Quiffe finishes aggressively fingering my vagina, which was rather painful to be honest, I'd never

24

had anything up there before. I didn't even know if I had a hole, well I tell ya, we made one after this! He straightens up and says.

Jack 'Right I'm going to make this simple. Give me a titty wank.'

Saoirse 'A titty wank?' [I says.]

Jack 'Yes.'

Saoirse [He says.]

Jack 'Give my cock a wank with your tits.'

Saoirse I nearly fucking died I was a thirty-two double-A, I'd no tits to wank him with! So he takes his trousers down and I pull my top up and shove my two fried eggs together. Burger nips, they used to call me. The nipples were bigger than the actual tit. And he whips out this chode of a thing. And starts trying to rub it up and down in between my tits.

But there's nothing there so he's just grinding on my sternum . . . And let me remind you, we're in a church car park, I'm going to hell for this if nothing else!

People are passing by so he turns me around to block his cock.

Jack 'Quick Saoirse hide my willy there goes the Bishop.'

Saoirse 'Evening Your Grace!'

And it doesn't take him very long, before I'm covered in his manly juices.

'Now what do I do?' [I says.]

'Father Mick is dropping me home!'

Jack 'I don't know.'

Saoirse [He says.]

Jack 'Sort yourself out, I'm heading back in to the lads.'

Saoirse 'You can't fucking leave me here.' [I says.]

'In a church car park, covered in cum.'

Jack 'See you later ye, got to run.'

Saoirse Don't worry Ashling, it's only hand sanitiser.

–

Mr Glynn's been teaching us how to put the numbers in the ledgers.

Mr Glynn 'Close your legs girls my eyes are wandering.'

Aoife Kelly 'What are you looking up our skirts for Sir?'

Saoirse Aoife Kelly says. So he gets taken out of class. And then a few days later he's allowed back in! And she is moved to a different class . . . Is that what actually happened? Do you remember that Ashling?

Ashling Ye he did it a lot.

Mr Glynn 'Put your jumpers on girls your shirts are see-through.'

Saoirse Ugh. So, a few months later, I'm standing opposite my sister Daisy in the dress rehearsal of the school play, and I'm wearing fake balls. I take this really seriously – I need to know what this would feel like.

Something empowering about this, I don't know what but I like using the bellow and taking up this much space. This is more feckin fun than I thought it'd be.

Mrs Toad 'Saoirse tone it down a bit!'

Saoirse Mrs Toad says, So I give it even more.

(*Overly RP.*) 'You there!'

Mrs Toad 'Just, *you there.*'

Saoirse (*overly RP*) 'You there!'

Antigone's after burying her brother.

'You there, studying the ground, hold up your head and tell us, is this true?' And by the time of the performance in front of the entire school, I realise this is feckin brilliant, I am commanding the stage here.

–

And I never want to come out of this role, it makes me feel alive Ashling.

(*Whispered on voice.*) And I'm in the wings and I hear the pupils taking their seats and I know my mum and Father Mick are somewhere in the audience.

The adrenalin flooded in Daisy; she's playing Antigone. But me, I'm as cool as a cucumber! Because I think everyone will only be looking at her as she's playing the broken-ish woman, in a pretty dress. And then I realise, this is the most real I've ever felt, playing Creon, thank you Sophocles.

And just before the house lights go down it hits me. This is just a part. So it's never going to be enough. So I say a quick Hail Mary and I'm thinking about being able to walk about so freely, chin high, head higher, chest open, stance wide, not feel like a prisoner in a ship never shown, how to use its own . . . But sailing freely, and what that might be like here in Enniskerry, to hold the gaze of a male and be the last to look away . . . And the lights come up and I can't stop imagining my life in another way . . . So I relish in the moment of:

'You there! Did you or did you not know that the proclamation forbade all this?'

And Mrs Toad is sighing, and in walks titty wank, and I notice Sister Patricia here and Mr Glynn too.

So I grab my balls and I hold them high.

And Daisy is just staring at me.

'Do you have any idea what you have done to our women?'

And no one has a clue I've gone off script. But Daisy's laid down pretending to be a corpse. 'You must trust your intuition girls, before they teach you to forget.'

–

'And the girls are screaming!'

'Father Mick over here.' [I says.] 'He's as reverent as they come and he has a secret wife! You heard me, and Mr Glynn at the back's a perv and Aoife Kelly was made the villain which she of course accepted, because we are *deeply conditioned!*'

And Sister Patricia is mouthing.

Sister Patricia '*Staaaaaaaaaannnd-dooowwwwn!*'

Sound and lighting have now switched to last year's pantomime.

Saoirse 'And Jack at the back made me wank his cock, and the Sister here.'

Daisy Leave me out of this!'

Saoirse 'Not you Daisy – Blessed Patricia. Who I asked to show us how, denied my request, so I was left with cum on my chest. And I would like to know as the King here, because apparently that gives me *basic human fucking rights*, what will the compensation be for the business ledger that Mr Glynn has made me forget how to do? Because my body is triggered by the sight, the sound, the touch of, his sin.'

And I've ignited Daisy, she is up from the dead – fire in her eyes.

Daisy 'And I, have polycystic ovaries, and I want to know why I haven't been taught about more roles for women in the history books, because surely they were fucking around.'

Saoirse 'And I fucking second that! In the kingdom here on earth, that is here for us to view. If you taught us in the classroom, so we didn't have to rub them out in the loo.'

–

Ashling Saoirse Murphy! I still can't believe you did that on our school stage.

Saoirse Yeye Ash, it was feckin different every night. In another life, no – I got expelled.

Ashling Ye and they never let you back in Saoirse.

Saoirse Ye I know. [I says.] And you were out too.

–

You remember my final day at school? I came in to collect all my stuff. We thought it was so normal to just not go. Or did we? Anyway, Orla's lurking in the lockers. Our relationship was one of those fluid ones. Orla loved the tickles as well. Mind you I was still only attracted to women by this point, I just hadn't a feckin clue!

Orla 'Quick up to the holy room, you up for it?'

Saoirse [Orla says.] 'Up for what?' [I says.]

Orla 'Let's scissor each other's legs before you go.'

Saoirse 'Oh right, why not!'
    And so we go up to the holy space. And she's a shoulder of vodka for me as a leaving present.
    So I down some and we hoist our skirts up.

Choral music blares serendipitous from an intercom.

And the morning prayers start ringing. So I am –

'Hail my Queen, I give you my,

my.'

Just on the cusp of –

And in walks Sister Patricia as Orla says.

Orla 'Stick your finger in my asshole, gently, if you're up for that?

NownowNOW.'

Saoirse And so *I collapse on top of Orla*. And I –

'Have you an underlying heart condition, or something, Orla?'

Orla 'Nono I just love your legs.'

Saoirse 'Oh, of course you do.' [I says.] 'That explains it, you were very, receptive, as I was resuscitating you. I thought: *is she really unconscious?* But you were.

Oh! Hello Sister Patricia!'

Sister Patricia 'Saoirse Murphy, Do you think I am some duck? You have been banned from the property!'

Saoirse 'Ye I know Sister, it was a complex procedure, stepping out. I thought, I'll go up to the holy room and mark the moment. And who do I meet on her deathbed? Orla! And the leak above, saturated Orla's. And the only thing, the only thing Sister. That brought her back to life, was the drip and *my kiss combined*. And then well you walked in so – you know, and we don't name the floods Sister. We follow the instinct of the drip, satiating in the, feckin nip.'

And she's out the door like a shot, and she comes charging back in with Mrs O'Heffer.

Mrs O'Heffer 'Saoirse Murphy, Sister Patricia informed me on what she walked in on! I should tell you, they have a view of those sorts of preferences. I know you're leaving but Orla. If you're staying. Be aware who you, talk to. Or do, that, with . . . Not on our premises.'

Saoirse And I leave, and the look on her face when I collected the final results.

'Straight A's.'

Mrs O'Heffer 'I don't know how you did it.'

Saoirse 'And an award for English and drama.'

I worked my hole off in the confines of my bedroom!

Mrs O'Heffer 'Saoirse, by the way, you can't be a lesbian. And I'll tell you why, lesbians don't have blonde hair; Mrs Foley our hockey teacher is one, and she has a different way, which is more *discreet* than you.'

–

Saoirse No wonder I wanted to emigrate after that, the shame made me ill.

Ashling Saoirse are you a lesbian?

Saoirse [You says.] I don't know. [I says.] I like vaginas, they're nicer lookin and more compact. I fucking hate the word lesbian, I wish it had a different name.

Ashling Like what?

Saoirse [You says.] Eh, like purple.

Ashling Purple?

Saoirse Yeye, your favourite colour. I'm a *purple*, that's nicer. I'm going to call myself *a purple*, Ashling.

–

By the end of that summer. It had been two months since I last made myself sick.

Ashling I'm so proud of you.

Saoirse [You says.] And it was the first time you'd worn your new wig out in public. Do you remember? I curled it for you and we made it look really nice.

And your sister dropped us to the Wicklow mountain and she told me that you had a granola bar in your bag and she'd love if you ate it. So I stop off at the corner shop and buy a big box of Celebrations to make you feel comfortable. Did you notice I did that? And your flip-flop falls off so I give you a piggyback and we reach the top. And the wind, it nearly takes the skin that's left off your face. Do you remember that Ashling?

Ashling Ye I was six stone.

Saoirse So I'm digging into my Celebrations to make you feel at ease. And you actually took out the granola bar, I couldn't believe it because I'd never seen you eat before. I barely looked at you but I was giving you the sneaky side eye and digging into the Malteser flavours. Is that why you ate the bar? And I didn't want to make a thing of it, so we sit in silence for a bit.

I'm so proud of you! [I says.]

Ashling I'm going to get better.

Saoirse [You says.] And a little while later, you took your top off and you showed me what you'd done.

Saoirse draws a crucifix on her chest with red lipstick.

You showed me that you'd carved a crucifix into your chest, I never said this to you but that really affected me.

And I didn't really know how to deal with the situation so. I walk away and I wish I had more patience with you. And you follow me and you tell me all the reasons I deserve love, for all the healing I'm doing, why my life is worth living. And I felt so helpless because it was you who needed – We both did.

And I am out of options so. I need to tell you something. [I says.]

I'm moving to Musical Theatre School in England at the end of the summer.

Ashling Why do you need to go away?

Saoirse [You says.]

Ashling Just stay here, or I could come.

Saoirse And it's making me sad because you're sad.

Don't cry, I just need to go.

And you leave.

You can't walk home from here, it'll take you hours, Ashling.

Ashling I need to burn off the calories.

Saoirse Just stop for a minute. [I says.] And I tell you, if Aoife Kelly could get better then so can you.

Ashling Aoife's anorexia wasn't as bad as mine.

Saoirse That's not the point. [I says.] She was going deaf and blind and now she's recovered. And you don't back down so I let it go, and I wish I knew the right thing to say. And then we stopped for a while. Do you remember that Ashling? That was around the time you went back into hospital and they started force-feeding you. I know you hated them sticking the tubes in you but I was so relieved because it was the only thing keeping you alive. And then I head off to Musical Theatre School in England. You really didn't want me to go.

Ashling Saoirse Murphy.

Saoirse [You says.]

Ashling I don't think Musical Theatre School will be good for your eating disorder.

Saoirse Well I can tell you something Ashling Daly, you were so feckin right. But I left, and I started this new life in England and I never told anyone about anything,

and I was fine.

–

Act Two

Beth (*Essex accent*) 'Are you alright babe?'

Saoirse They says. 'Am I alright?' [I says.]

Anna 'Yes babe! You okay?'

Saoirse An Essex person's way of saying, how are you . . . Conas atá tú, Ashling.

'Ye I'm fine, why? Do I look sad?' And then I almost feel sad cuz they're asking!

'Are you alright?' [I says.]

Maria 'Ye babe!'

Saoirse England.

Lighting and sound for a dance performance.

And the girls are chanting.

'If you want to be a dancer you've got to trim your thighs, if you want to be a dancer you've got to trim your thighs.'

Saoirse 'That's just the body dysmorphia.' I tell them: 'Your thighs are absolutely fine.'

Maria 'Nono.'

Saoirse They says.

Maria 'The weigh-in lady after ballet says it.'

Saoirse And they're all measuring each other's waists with tapes and eating lettuce. I on the other hand, am still playing men, and so I'm writing an email to the head because I'm sick of it.

Glitzy Principal (*smoking*) 'You'll have a big part end of year love, trust me.'

Saoirse 'And will I play a real woman?' And I tell her: 'I need to make it here, please, I cannot go back. So I need you to let me play the brokenest, most distraught woman so they can see, I can play all the roles that get written / for women.'

Glitzy Principal 'Broken woman? You'll be playing the strongest woman love. This is your training.'

Saoirse And I don't fucking understand because I'm in the balls again. And I was going for Juno not Jack the Paycock! So I'm stood in rehearsals, hair tucked under my cap and I'm wearing a handsome suit. And I have a massive crush on my friend Maria, she's playing my wife. And I realise what it might be like. God, I'd be so much kinder than the lads were back home. 'The whole world's in a terrible state of chassis.' [He says.] And he's right.

Beth 'Chassis. Are these Irish musicals?'

Saoirse Nono plays. And they're also teaching us how to play consent for roles, in shows. Can you believe it? Thank you Jesus!

Feck. Fecckk! Feckfeckfeck.

Sound of Skype ringing.

And it's your birthday Ash – I know I'm a day late. They didn't have twenty, so I put in eighty-three.

Saoirse sticks '8' and '3' candles in a cake. She lights them, singing.

Lá breithlá shona duit, lá breithlá shona duit, lá breithlá shona duit!

Happy twentieth birthday! Blow from Ireland. Come on ya granny! Make a wish.

She blows them out.

Well my wish is to remember the female body, at every age and stage.

Because I think they should be made holy.

Will I go to hell for saying that? Joke.
    Oh feck I might, sorrysorry.

Sorry!
    No! I'm not feckin sorry, I've been in hell, this. Is what hell is.

What's your wish Ashling?

> *Music interjects. Blackout. Lights up. Saoirse eyeballs the cake.*
> *Blackout. Lights up. Saoirse leans back on an edge. She struggles.*
> *Blackout. Lights up. Saoirse crouches down, in agony. Blackout. Lights up.*

Daisy 'I'm giving it a go at the Sisters of Mercy.'

Saoirse [Daisy says.]

Daisy 'I can't have children so I might as well give it to God.'

Saoirse 'Fair play to ye.' [I says.]

And so I fly home and next thing I know, we're all sat in this massive hall.

These institutions are minted Ashling. The amount of people making donations, hoping to save their souls when their souls are fine. Someone should tell them! Now I've had three gin and tonics and Daisy's wearing a lovely suit.

'You're a feckin ride.'

And the new sisters are being welcomed and the head of the pack gets up.

Reverend Mother 'Most promising sister in training, for her work in inner-city Dublin and indeed with the elderly here in our own district; goes to, Daisy Murphy.'

Saoirse And she's up, she's giving a speech!

Daisy gets out a microphone and settles into the sound of her amplified voice.

Daisy 'Gosh! Thank you, so much.

This is a real honour.

I guess I'd, ye.

I'd really like to lead a mass one day.

So, this prize is dedicated to that. Is that okay to say?
Yeah!
Ye it is.

And put us in suits. Not the dresses, it's the twenty-first century and they just feel a bit, century.

I urge you to empower us,

thank you.'

Saoirse (*manically*) 'Well done Daisy. Fucking excellent. She's my sister!'

I'm off my tits so I'm escorted out to the loo by Father Mick. Bear in mind it's a very quiet occasion. Not many were invited but because of his, perks of the patriarch, the holy fam made it in. And I meet an older woman, Jacinta and she tempts me into town for an after party. So we leg it through the halls, past my mum and Father Mick! And I plant a big kiss on Jacinta.

Brenda 'Oh Saoirse, not here love.'

Saoirse Mum says. But the whole formality sort of makes it, impossible not to. And I end up at some after party and I have a threesome with.

'Hello Jacinta.'

And some man with crocodile eyes!

'Jacinta.' [I says.] 'Are you allowed to do this kind of thing?'

Jacinta 'I've not been initiated yet Saoirse and you, well you could turn me!'

Saoirse 'Turn you from? Oh.'

And the next day, Daisy's a bit perplexed.

Daisy 'Saoirse are you gay? Jacinta O'Reilly said you took her to places she's never been before.'

Saoirse 'Did she?'

Daisy 'Ye, can you not see I want to have a real go at this Saoirse?'

Saoirse 'Yeye no problem.' [I says.] 'And I've been calling myself a purple here, because sometimes, I just don't want to define it at all.'

Do you remember that Ashling? Or did we ever talk about that? And I'm feeling manic from the comedown of it all, so I decide to tell my mother all about it:

'And then I just licked it, sorry.
    What would you say Mum?
    Went down on her?
    Eh, lick-out
    I licked
    her out,
    Mum.
    I
    personally
    find them too tickly,
    so I give them.'

Brenda (*stunned*) 'Oh, right. Okay, very-good-Saoirse. We won't tell Father Mick. *And we don't talk like this in public spaces!*'

Saoirse 'Why not?' [I says.] 'The boys do.'

–

I'm back in England and I have BDSM with Otillie.

Ashling Her name is Otillie?

Saoirse Yes Ashling it means prosperous in battle, she told me while we were fucking.

Otillie 'Bondage Sadomasochism!'

Saoirse [She says.] Flagellating, they did it for years in the brothers; it can be quite an act of *kink*.

Classical music plays.

'What are these for?'

I ask her, as she strokes her canes and whips and chains.

Otillie 'To tie you from the ceiling.'

Saoirse [She says.] 'Oh right, very good.'

I nearly feckin died. She's older than me, a graduate – and she's giving me a tour of her flat and her hand is on my lower back. So we start with the fridge. The coolest water, in bottles – *from Ocado*. With pink flowers on the front!

And the ice cream is *freezing*, *minty* – Vegan. And the snacks are spicy, and the pizza is. Extra *doughy* but gluten-*free*! And before we know where we are, a living-room floor has never felt more appealing. And this is like nothing I've ever experienced! Till she says:

Otillie 'I had a dream you slept with my neighbour.'

Saoirse 'Oh, what the fuck were you dreaming about us for?'

Oh maybe she's trying to be kinky, I read about this once.

'Okay, right. I fucked your neighbour . . . now what?'

And next thing I know, she's ordering four hundred pounds' worth of new toys. And I order a takeaway. Both arrive on express delivery! And I shouldn't have eaten so much because now I can't stay present. *And the body, here.* Which, if it wasn't such a place of *shame*. Might actually be *enjoyed*. So I'm thinking about how much I've, consumed. And random lines from *Juno and the Paycock*, are *floating* through my *periphery*, and I forget to call *the safe word*. So she's giving me a good hiding and I

am remembering the *woooooord.*

'Ah, stop stop. Mother of Mercy! Sorry I was thinking about. Ah, nono no biting. Oh! Okay . . .
   ye.'

And the pain makes me feel alive – like I'm here, like I'm present, I fucking love it. That was actually quite nice Ashling!

–

Music pulses in a club. Saoirse dances, wildly.

Sound cuts to the edge of a pier. She makes a phone call.

Hello Mum it's Saoirse Murphy.

What are you up to?

Yeye I know,
   I got the WhatsApp.

In a club, ye. Came out to.
   I don't / want. Ye. When?

She did / yeah.
   I tried.
   Went twice before and / tried again.

Do you know what?

Oh.

I don't know.

No, because I'm at the pier. Southend Pier, the water looks nicer in the dark. It's black, it's so nice.

What?

Nono, I'm not doing that any more Mum, I got the help book you sent me it was really
Helpful.

Red wine.

Half a glass?

I don't know if I'm coming, can you just drop it?

Please for the love of – ah for feck sake!

Sorry, yeye I will okay.

Love you too. Bye.

–

Pantomime lights and sound.

I'm doing the kids' panto in a library in Dagenham.
We carry the set in a feckin van Ashling!

–

And eh, ye. It's great. But you'll never guess what I did. We were running lines in the loo and I took too many.

I've never tried this before.

How do you open the bean bag? So I give it a good tug. And lo and behold. Snowflakes all over the place.

Snowflakes shower her.

Worse, it was all over our costumes. So there we were like feckin eejits. Sniffing it off each other's legs and arms. Shhhcoooooping it off the floor.

Sound of a loud thud.

Ow! Where did the iron gate come from?

Child 'Mummy what's Jack doing?'

Child's Mummy He's not well poppet, Jack is, sick.

Saoirse And the parents leave.
   'So I walk up to the giant's castle. And I leap down the stalk.
   'Hearyehearye! Oh yes I did, sorry wrong bit. Oh no it's not, oh yes it's not!'

–

'Where are you all going?
   My brain is tired Jack, the car needs petrol.
   And what happens – if you don't know where your car is?
   So I lay there for a while making angels in the snow.
   Where is everyone going? I'm having a party – Feckin pricks. Santa's NOT REAL!'

Ashling Saoirse.

Saoirse Sorry Ash / I.

Ashling Line your stomach.

Saoirse [You says.]

Ashling [Just go home.]

Saoirse Home? It's too late.

–

'Woooow – you look like St Patrick!
   He banished the snakes the feckin legend.'

The police officer's looking over me.

'And you know what Brigid did?'

43

Police Officer 'No?'

Saoirse 'Me neither.'

Police Officer 'Have you taken any drugs darlin?'

Saoirse 'No?'

Police Officer 'Do you take drugs?'

Saoirse 'No!'

She leans on him.

Police Officer 'We need to take you to hospital to look at the drugs in your system.'

Saoirse 'Ibuprofen, horse tranquillisers, Calpol, that sort of thing.'

[And he says.]

Police Officer 'We'll do a blood test.'

Saoirse 'Cocaine and tequila, and Calpol! I feckin love that one. The pink one.

Do you have any?

–

Don't look at me like this Officer.

I forget what I've come from, and that's the whole point, earth suit is a ball ache! And the emphasis, is on the ball.'

It's gas Ashling! We're all here in the back of the nee-naw.

'I won awards Officer and –
    I used to be really good at this.
    I just forgot how to . . .

Came before!

Heart wasn't connecting to.

44

Glorify in the.

In the.'

   Sound of hospital machines.

Nurse 'You can't be trying to take your own life.'

Saoirse The nurse says. 'I didn't?' And I'm trying to see clearly.
   But the room is spinning. And the chaplain has been called in and he's standing over my bed, like I've a pot of gold beneath me.

'Do you do BBQ spare ribs here? – Wow, you kind of look like Fred Astaire.

He's a tap-dancer!

You just reminded me of him there – the way you moved the tray.'

Hospital Chaplain 'We were giving you the last rites Saoirse.'

Saoirse [He says.]

'Oh right.
   I've always wanted those.'

And then she arrives.

'Mum!'

Followed by Daisy.

And around the corner.

My own father walks in Ashling!

–

'Dad.'

Brendan 'Saoirse what have you gotten yourself into now?'

Saoirse [He says.]

Brendan 'I've been living with monks near Rome. I love them as much as I love you, so I did it for all of us.'

Saoirse 'Daisy can you get me Doritos.'

Brendan 'Saoir saoir, are you okay?'

Saoirse 'You know Dad that's a trick question over here.'

Brendan 'You're not doing the puking thing any more are you?'

Saoirse 'Nono Dad of course not.'

Brendan 'Great, and well my only friend, Father Mick, who I know lives with your mother. He was the only one to have known about my walk with the monks. And he sent me a voice note on WhatsApp, to say you'd hit your head on a gate in a library in Dagenham. And from the wind through the blower, you were hooked up here the next day, weren't you?'

Saoirse 'Ye.'

Brendan 'Great.'

Brenda 'Saoirse.'

Saoirse Mum says.

Brenda 'If we are going to be paying your school fees. You, you. You can't be doing co-caine.'

Saoirse 'Gosh Mum would ye stop, it was only a one-off.'

Brendan 'No Saoirse, that is a class-A drug!'

Saoirse 'I like your hair Brendan, did you get it cut? It's lovely, you look like the Pope.'

Brendan 'Oh, thank you very much. On that note. I forgive you.'

Saoirse And here comes Daisy. She's brought Doritos Ashling, excellent. And this is awkward, Dad's crying.

Brendan 'Daisy! Are you having a baby? Or did you eat your way over?'

Saoirse She met a fisherman in São Paulo Ashling! So she left her training and now she's pregnant.

Brendan 'Saoirse! Is this because I left for the monks?'

Saoirse 'Well, it was a bit traumatic but like. You're here.'

Oh my God he's about to overshare.

Brendan 'I live with monks, near Rome.'

Saoirse 'We heard you the first time.'

Brendan 'So, we all feel a bit, responsible do we? For Saoirse being, the way she is.'

Saoirse Rude.

Nurse 'Oh no.'

Saoirse [The nurse says.]

Nurse 'We use the three Cs here – we didn't *cause* anyone's disease. We can't *control* anyone's disease. And we can't *cure* anyone's disease.'

Saoirse 'I don't believe that I have a disease.' [I says.]

'I am dis-eased by this situation, yes. And the only thing I have to control my voided existence . . .

Is a blanket of chaos, it keeps me alive – to take it off would be too real.

She gets up.

You ran away to join a closet Brendan, why do you judge mine?

And I don't need anyone to tell me how I should, or shouldn't play roles. Or how I should or shouldn't internalise all the homophobia. But what if I didn't want to call myself a purple? Or can I not be a lesbian because I have blonde hair? Who made that rule? And I am so fed up of this giant fucking voice, hardwired in my head. So that a world based on balls-only constructs, can remain enforcing rules on the body, *basic human rights*. But who's to say that some people in this world aren't worthy of piety? Or connection to something greater, than this? We all live here! It's one of the biggest atrocities known – to humankind.'

And yet calling it, naming it, well that opens up shit for them. But we never knew all of this, did we Ashling? But this here it's like I'm living, but I'm dead. I am shot to pieces, and I carry on.

Brendan 'Saoirse!'

Saoirse [Dad says.]

Brendan 'You sound pro-found. And I know *I taught you how to read*.'

Daisy 'Brendan! I wouldn't.'

Saoirse [Daisy says.] 'And I am so used to making everything into a fairytale! Because this, is the only way, to make sense of the chaos. This is too much to go into for a hangover. Can you knock me out? Do you do that here?'

And I've downed the Doritos, Ashling. And I don't do what I normally do, I just take it all in.

Brendan 'I'm so sorry, love.'

Saoirse [Brendan says.]

Brendan 'It was the shame. I guess we wear it as a nation. So, I needed to get away.

I'm so.

So.

Proud of you, Saoirse.'

Brenda 'We all are.'

Saoirse 'Thanks lads. Thank you.'

–

Festive sounds.

I'm back in Ireland for Christmas Ashling and Daisy's about to give birth.

Brendan 'Were there many at my fake funeral?'

Saoirse [Dad says.]

Brendan 'Come on, tell me who went and, who didn't. Oh I'd love to have been a fly on the wall.'

Saoirse And Father Mick and the Bishop are all around the table – for the modern family dinner.

Brendan 'Father P is now a bishop.'

Saoirse [Dad says.]

Brendan 'So don't talk about the hijinks in Dagenham.'

Saoirse 'He's seen my tits Dad so I think we're past that!'

Brendan 'Excuse me?'

Saoirse 'Yeye! No problem Brendan.'

Daisy 'My own are lactating.'

Saoirse [Daisy says.]

Daisy 'Mind you I don't miss shoving Tampax up once a month and I know my anus might rip from the birth and I'm okay with that.'

Saoirse And Ashling, it was the best moment of my life.

'You might poo too, so feckin what like. You're birthing a human, women are feckin amazing.'

So Father Mick's gone green here! And Mum's bringing the starters. I don't know about you Ashling, but I've always dreaded the Christmas holidays. All the different types of food, Mother of God. The potatoes alone – *Mashedpotato-boiledpotato-rosemaryroastedpotato-potatowedges-jacketpotato-potatosalad-sweetpotato-frenchfries-leakandpotatogratin!*

Nothing compares to the guilt I felt when I stood up to go to the toilet after the dinner.

Daisy 'Saoirse, Mum's turkey was eighty euro. And for you to puke that all back up – You selfish fucking cunt. Sorry. Hormones!'

Saoirse So, up to the toilet I go. Puke it all back up and then straight back down for round two. This was on a loop Ashling, I was out of control! Meringues-strawberry cheesecake chocolate cheesecake pavlova *fruitcake* honeycombicecream-vanillaicecream-chocolatefudgebrownies-chocolatebiscuitcake-FERRERO ROCHER!

Ashling Did you keep the dessert down?

Saoirse [You says.] The look in my sister's soft, sad eyes.

Brief sounds of a lullaby.

Daisy 'Please.'

Saoirse But even that couldn't stop the urge to purge. So I went up to my bedroom, and I puked in a Dunnes Stores bag. Even though I knew it had been too long and the calories would have definitely absorbed into my blood by now. So, to get rid of any extras. I mix some Epsom salts in water, down them in one. Fucking rotten they are. And wait for them to kick in. And for the explosions out me arse to start. But just to be sure. To be-sure, tobesure. TOBESURE.

Seasonal music, Saoirse works out, it ends in collapse.
She stands up, eventually.

–

So I'm back at college Ashling and I'm making myself sick around, twelve times a day. Think I've eroded my oesophagus away now, because I get sick without even sticking my fingers down my throat. I'm completely dead and gone inside now. And I feel like my soul has left my body. And I'm just floating through life somewhere. And when people try to speak to me, they're just speaking to my remains, it's really weird. I don't know if this makes sense Ashling. This started just after you died actually.

Ashling I died?

–

Saoirse [You says.] Ye.

–

But I pretended in my head that you didn't and we carried on having our conversations. And I remember getting the WhatsApp from Aoife Kelly.
   Ashling Daly died, I remember the shock. You couldn't have died Ashling, you were going to live.

And my best friends from Musical Theatre School were all holding me. Maria, Anna and Beth.

–

All holding me and stroking my head.

Maria 'I'm so sorry Saoirse.'

Anna 'I'm so sorry.'

Saoirse They kept saying, and I fell onto the bar in the nightclub in Southend, and I couldn't even cry for a while. I wasn't really present after that, I wasn't really present for a long time after that. I went home the next day for your funeral and I watched you being lowered into the ground, *Ashling Daly*, written on your gravestone. *Died, aged twenty.*

Ashling I'm still twenty.

Saoirse [You says.]

Ashling I'll always be twenty.

Saoirse Do you remember those stories I used to tell you, to make you excited about living? The stories about fighting with Sister Patricia, and playing Creon in the school play, and BDSM with Otillie . . . did I ever tell you them?

I keep replaying them over and over in my head.

I'm just trying to pinpoint where I lost you, and then you says . . .

Well I don't know what you would say.

I'm sorry I wasn't there for you. I'm sorry I wasn't there to help you eat more granola bars.

I'm sorry I didn't know the right things to say.

I'm sorry I left you behind.

Music plays.

–

Act Three

Lights and sounds of a garden in spring.

Saoirse A few years later, after I played Pope Joan. I come back to Ireland to take a look. Mum, Dad and Father Mick are all heading off to Rome. Maybe they're just openly reforming the church.

'Polyamorous lads?'

Brendan 'No Saoirse!'

Saoirse 'Oh the weather's better over, is it? I see the benefits!' And I start to do really well and I make my offer for the family home. Paid for it outright.

'That is my final offer.' And I turn it into a sisterhood. A freedom dream. *SaoirseAisling*. Spelt the way it means – but sounding like planting your spirit here, too. This is where we rest.

And I tell everyone about playing Pope Joan. She was the woman who had to pretend to be a man. And then I realised, that's what I've been doing. I've been trying to understand who I feel like, and I've come home to myself. And home today, is wherever I am.

And Pope Joan gave birth during a Papal procession.

Pope Joan holds her baby in her arms. She gives a blessing in Latin.

Pope Joan 'Lupus pilum sed non vitium perdit.'

Saoirse Meaning the wolf sheds his pelt but not his characteristically vicious behaviour. And ever since they have a testicle chair, designed like a loo for the genitalia to be examined. If you've balls you're a pope and if you've ovaries, you're not. But here in this house, everyone's welcome.

And we practise stepping into big roles like Taoiseach, President, Cardinal and we also, teach consent. And my niece and goddaughter, Gabriella sits beside me. Her Communion was yesterday, Ashling. So this is the afters. Like feckin weddings these things. And Mum's last Sunday roast.

Brenda 'Saoí sios, sit down.'

Saoirse [She says.] And Gabby is up on her chair.

Daisy's child, Gabriella, stands tall.

Gabriella 'Before we eat.'

Saoirse [She says.]

Gabriella 'I am not seen in church, the way the boys are,
    which means I am not seen in my country, the way the
boys are, which means I am not seen in this man-made
world, so how do I know I am seen in Heaven?'

Saoirse I feckin love this child! 'Are you the next Oscalina Wildina?'

[And she says.]

Gabriella 'This is what we wrote after the compassion for the dresses.'

Saoirse 'We learnt the word yesterday.' [I says.] [And she says.]

Gabriella 'Yeno . . .? When Tom Brady wanted to wear my,
Communion dress, and I wanted to wear, the priest's dress,
    and none of us got to wear what we wanted,
    so we were left with nothing but . . .
    money.

And that's not fair, because Tom Brady made more money off his Communion than me . . .

Most of the boys made more money than the girls . . . like a trick the church is playing on us.

Was it in the rule book for Communions???

Because I didn't know I was going to make less money for being a girl . . .

So I have loads of compassion for myself.'

Saoirse And Mum's jaw has hit the floor.

Brenda 'Jesus tonight! That's a brilliant way of putting it. I've never made as much as your grandad and I do all the work around here.'

Saoirse And I look round the table.

Gran in the centre.

And Gabriella

our own angel child . . . And Daisy's lost her mind.

Daisy 'Saoirse! Stop telling everyone she's an angel. The teacher has been writing home thinking she's off her feckin head!'

Saoirse And we spend the evening in the garden making wishes.

End.

SHOWER

This short film is dedicated to
all bereaved during the Covid pandemic
and to all the healthcare workers too.

With love and thanks to Denise.

Shower was first screened as part of the Abbey Theatre's *Dear Ireland* season on 28 April 2021. Aoife was played by Denise Gough.

Characters

Aoife

Shower. Early morning.

Aoife has just come back from a shift in ICU. She is a nurse.

Aoife Yeah it's dripping. Split-second intervals.

Light brown.

Not quite brown bread brown, half wholemeal.

Constant drip now like a long *ssss*. I've bandaged it with tape round the.

Whaddya call it yeno that thing.

The pole, tube.

You know the long stick thing.

The PIPE, yes the pipe. It's not my apartment.

How much will it cost?

–

Right, how soon can you get here?

–

I start shift then, can you come any earlier?

–

I'll leave a key under the mat.

Thank you.

You have a very Irish name for an Englishman. We have a whole brand of tea in your name, Barry!

I'd murder a cup.

–

It's exhausting.
    People can't be with their loved ones at the end yeno.

Very hard.
    Just now an elderly lady. I held her hand

–

It's my job, like you plumbin we're all just doing our jobs!

–

Not easy, no Barry you're right!

Not as easy as this water is finding its way out its hole –
more of a dark brown bread colour now.

Like a pooish colour sorry I've a three-year-old we talk
about poo a lot.

–

Yeah.
    I haven't seen them in weeks.

We've a fifteen-year-old too who is very angry at her mum,
which is joyful.

I'd do anything for a long shower, they help me wash the
day away.

You couldn't pop up in the next hour?

–

I understand.

I've put a whaddya call it a, what are they called.

A bucket! Underneath.

If it keeps going I reckon I could bathe in it!

I'd probably be able to sit in it.

We jumped off the Forty Foot at Christmas.

I'd love to jump in there right now.

–

Well I thought about going back to Ireland to help but England's raised me too so I feel conflicted.

And a bit of shame around that, actually.
    My heart is in Ireland but my feet are in England. I got to be where my feet are.

I'm staying *here*. I love Ireland my heart will always be there but, we've stopped Barry the drip has come to a halt is that good or bad?

–

What would we do without you, Barry you're a hero.

Well, just being on the phone is nice. My friend left your number on the side.

BARRY THE PLUMBER!

Here's one for ye, what country eats the most cornflakes in the world?

–

Give it a guess. No, Ireland!

–

Yeah.
    Hang on hang on text from my daughter:

'Dad's made shitty salty ribs for the sixth night in a row. I've become a vegetarian.'

She's at that age.
    She doesn't like me being away.

No no, yeah she's high risk it's a yeah, a.
Mm Mm Mm.
Eh.
Mm.

–

A shower would be perfect.
My skin feels like it might fall off you know those feckin

suits they have us in I reckon I'm losing ten pounds a day
just the heat of them alone, running round.

And a tea, but I've no running water and a leaky pipe!
Blinding headache too, the goggles.
Oh, Ciara, hang on:

'Mum you didn't buy cornflakes.'

That's great isn't it Barry? Just what you want to hear. She's
calling. Stay there.

–

Hello Ciara,

–

I know I know baby why don't you watch a movie.
Yeah, a nice one.

–

Could you say a prayer?
No sorry sorry sorry Jesus, okay –
Are you wearing a coat?

–

Good girl, I know.

–

You're doing brilliantly.

–

Not long I promise.

–

Yes we can Skype I'm just on to the plumber darling and
I've work again in a few hours.
I'll Skype you as soon as I can okay?
Love you too.

Okay. Bye bye.

Aoife puts her earpiece back in.

Barry you still there?

Thank God, we've stopped dripping but the pipe is
pulsating.

–

She's grand. Do you've kids?
    Spoke too soon we're dripping again we're back to the
drip.

More of a clear colour looks, drinkable.

–

No no I won't, it just looks refreshing.

It has its own little heartbeat, pulsing pipes!

Oh Barr-rrrry Boy, the pipes the pipes are calling – come fix
my pipes or I'll jump out the windowwww, I want a hug
but nobody will touuucccchh me –

I'm delirious, can you tell?

–

The lady who passed today, Gale, lovely dear sweet Gale –
she had an underlying heart condition. Made me think of
Ciara.

Don't know when I'll see her next.

Her family FaceTimed.

Gale's.

I found her iPad and they said their goodbyes. That's rare, usually there's not enough time.

Hold my mum's hand, that's what her daughter kept saying to me.

'Please please please just hold my mum's hand. Hold her.'

I held her.
    I didn't let go till a long while after.

–

I'm just doing my job –
    We're dripping again.

    Aoife checks her phone again. She reads out another text.

'Mum I'm watching an eighteens movie, Dad said I could, what's the Netflix password?'

Whaddya reckon Barry do I give her the password?

Good idea.

    Aoife texts aloud as she types.

Ask, your, father.

She doesn't usually speak to me this much, it's like we're all coming out of isolation *in* isolation.

I'm honoured. Spoke too soon!

    Aoife reads another text.

'You ruin my life.'

The bitch.
    Sorry.
    I didn't mean that.

–

THESE GODDAMN PIPES!

–

Uh thanks you're very good.

–

Thanks for staying on the phone.
    Thanks for listening. You're very good.

–

Yeah I'll get some sleep.

–

Think I have a pasta pot.

–

Oh nonono honestly I'm grand for food.

–

Are you sure? Number forty-eight. Thank you.

    Aoife turns the tap on. The water flows freely.
We're suckin diesel Barry!

–

    Aoife breaks down.